MACMILLAN READERS

STARTER LEVEL

PHILIP PROWSE

L. A. Detective

macmillan education

Macmillan Readers is a series of engaging narrative texts designed to stimulate learners while enhancing their language skills, building literacy and boosting reading confidence. Through captivating stories and fascinating cultural themes, learners will explore a diversity of scenarios that foster vocabulary expansion, comprehension skills and a lifelong love of reading.

The right reader at every stage

Tailored to each learner's stage of language proficiency, our six levels feature text adapted to match the skill level. With controlled vocabulary and grammar, learners can read freely and immerse themselves in the story. When more challenging words are introduced, either the text will provide sufficient context to aid understanding or a full explanation will be provided in the Glossary.

Readers for all, anywhere, anytime

Macmillan Readers are perfect for shared, guided and independent reading. Whether in traditional print, immersive audio or the convenient eBook, Macmillan Readers are equally effective for in-class activities, paired discussions or solo reading at home or on the move.

Reading for pleasure, knowledge and well-being

Regular reading and reading for pleasure:

- increases reading confidence, benefiting all literacy skills, not just reading.
- reinforces and enriches vocabulary, providing a variety of contexts.
- expands general knowledge.
- supports concentration, inner reflection and well-being.

Macmillan Readers will inspire a love for reading in English while nurturing essential language skills. Unlock new worlds, expand horizons and embark on an adventure in English!

(NOTE: *While the content of Macmillan Readers is evaluated for age suitability, we kindly remind parents and teachers that they are ultimately responsible for determining whether a particular book is appropriate for their child or student.)*

MON
29
My name is Lenny Samuel. My friends call me Len. I'm a detective. I work in Los Angeles. I'm an L.A. detective.
Everybody in Los Angeles is busy. But Len isn't busy. He's sitting in his office. He's waiting. He has no work today. Nothing is happening.

Then a man comes into the office. Len doesn't know him. The man is short and dark. He's about forty years old. He's wearing a suit.
The man is holding a gun. The gun is pointing at Len.
I'm Frank. Come with me. Mr Blane wants to speak to you.
I won't go with you, Frank. I don't like Mr Blane. I don't want to speak to him.

Frank is a tough man. He laughs. He hits Len on the head. He hits Len hard. Len's eyes close. Len falls down. He falls onto the floor of the office.
82
PRIVATE
DETECTIVE
L. SAMUEL

Len wakes up. He opens his eyes. He's sitting in a big chair. The room is very warm. There are lots of plants in the room.
Where am I?
Hello, Mr Samuel. Welcome to my house.
An old man is talking and smiling. He's Mr Blane. He's a very rich man. He's also a very bad man.

You're going to help me, Mr Samuel. You're going to find my daughter. Read these letters.
CARMEN IS OUR PRISONER. WE WANT $100 000. GIVE US THE MONEY. THEN CARMEN WILL COME HOME. MEET US ON TUESDAY AT 2pm. MEET US AT THE BUS STATION. The Young Ones
Father, Help! Please give them the money. Carmen
Carmen is eighteen. She has long, dark hair. Her eyes are blue. She's beautiful.

Mr Blane gives Len a photo. He says, 'I want Carmen back. Go to the bus station at two o'clock on Tuesday. Frank has the $100 000. He's going with you. Give the money to The Young Ones. Bring Carmen home. I'll pay you $1000.'
Len says, 'I don't like you, Blane. I don't want your money. But Carmen is in trouble. She needs help. I'll help her.'

It's 2 pm on Tuesday. Frank and Len are at the bus station. Frank has $100 000 in a bag.
SAN FRANCISCO
Large buses are going in and out of the bus station. There are lots of people. But Len can't see Carmen.

Frank and Len wait. Then they see Carmen. She's standing by a bus. A young man is with her. The young man is holding Carmen's arm.
Hello. Are you Carmen Blane? I'm working for your father.
Who are you?
I'm from the Young Ones.

Frank opens the bag. The young man sees the money. The young man lets go of Carmen's arm.

Len holds Carmen's arm. Frank gives the bag of money to the young man.

Suddenly, Carmen bites Len's hand.
Len lets go of Carmen's arm.

The young man hits Frank.
Frank falls down.

Carmen and the young man jump onto the bus. The door of the bus closes. The bus drives off. It's going to San Francisco.
SAN FRANCISCO
Len can't get on the bus. He decides to get his car. Len decides to drive to San Francisco.

Len is in his car. He's driving to San Francisco. He's going to find Carmen.
101
Why is Carmen going to San Francisco? Who is the young man?

It's Thursday. Len is in San Francisco. San Francisco is a big city. Len can't find Carmen.

Suddenly, Len sees a sign on a building.

The sign says: The Young Ones. The building is a school for poor children. Carmen is playing with the children.

Len stops his car. He goes to speak to Carmen.

I don't want to go home. I'm happy here. I like working at this school. The $100 000 is for the school. My father is a bad man. These papers show he is a criminal. Take the papers to the police.
You stay here. Nobody will find you. I'll take the papers to the police. Good luck.

It's Friday. Len is in Los Angeles. He's at the police station. Frank and Blane are at the police station too.
NOT
These papers show that you're a criminal, Blane.
I'm tired. I have no money. But I have an exciting job. And I like to help people. That's why I'm an L.A. detective.

Macmillan Education Limited
4 Crinan Street
London N1 9XW

Companies and representatives throughout the world

Macmillan Readers Starter L.A. Detective
ISBN: 978-1-035-15124-0
Macmillan Readers Starter L.A. Detective with eBook and Resources
ISBN: 978-1-035-15127-1

First published 1993
This edition published 2024

Illustrated by John Richardson
Cover illustration by Mark Oldroyd

Printed and bound in Brazil
2025
2